AF207220

DILEMMAS

WHAT WOULD YOU DO?

DILEMMAS

WHAT WOULD YOU DO?

James Saywell and Anne-Marie Roffi

A Perigee Book

A Perigee Book
Published by The Berkley Publishing Group
A division of Penguin Putnam Inc.
375 Hudson Street
New York, New York 10014

First edition: July 2001

Published simultaneously in Canada.

The Penguin Putnam Inc. World Wide Web site address is
www.penguinputnam.com

Library of Congress Cataloging-in-Publication Data

Saywell, James
    Dilemmas : what would you do? / by James Saywell, Anne-Marie Roffi.
        p.   cm.
    ISBN 0-399-52681-1
        1. Ethical problems   I. Roffi, Anne-Marie.   II. Title.
BJ1031 .S28   2001
170—dc21

2001016315

Printed in the United States of America

10 9 8 7 6 5 4 3 2 1

Anne-Marie would like to dedicate this book to her parents.

Introduction

The book began with a dilemma . . .
that provoked heated discussions and sleepless nights . . .
that sparked other dilemmas . . .
that made us laugh . . .
that made us question our motivations . . .
that made us seek ulterior motives . . .
that triggered other dilemmas . . .
that made us doubt and humbled us . . .
that made us angry and frustrated . . .
that challenged us . . .
that led to other dilemmas . . .
that surprised us . . .
that taught us about ourselves and each other . . .

Life is a succession of dilemmas.
Handle them with care.

DILEMMAS

WHAT WOULD **YOU** DO?

You've started dating a woman and discover
she used to be a man.

One night, you're awakened by loud shouting, banging and screaming coming from your neighbors' house. You don't know them very well at all.

For the third night in a row, you're awakened by neighbors having an incredibly loud and violent argument.

The next-door neighbors' tree sheds half its leaves on your garage roof and garden.

Your neighbors regularly sunbathe nude in their garden.

The neighbors grow pot in their garden.

The neighbors' dog doesn't stop howling whenever it's left alone in the house.

You witness your neighbors constantly abusing their pet.

You suspect that the neighbors physically abuse their children.

You see someone cheating during an exam.

You see a friend cheating during an exam.

You're accused of cheating during an exam, because a friend asked you for help.

You realize that you could win a scholarship by altering a small detail on your application form.

A friend applying for the same job as you tells you he doctored his résumé.

A colleague you don't like at all falsified his résumé, but you find out by snooping through his desk.

Your teenager is applying to colleges, but has difficulty expressing himself in written form. He asks you to write his college entrance essay for him. You know that it would greatly improve his chances.

A friend applying for a job asks you to write a reference for him pretending he has worked at your office.

A friend who is a terrible driver
asks to borrow your car.

You lend someone a music CD. When you get it back, it skips.

A friend borrows a dress for a party and returns it with a stain on it.

You lend someone your car. When it's returned, you notice a dent on the side.

A week before your wedding, your husband's best man dies. Over a hundred people are coming, some from abroad.

On the eve of your wedding day, your husband's best man dies.

A week before your wedding, you get chicken pox.

Your wedding dress arrives the day before your wedding, and it doesn't fit.

The wrong wedding dress arrives the day before your wedding. Instead of the long white gown you were expecting, a short, sexy one arrives.

You and your pregnant wife have been invited to dinner at a colleague's house. Everyone starts talking about potential names for the baby and out of politeness you suggest the name of the host's baby. To your horror, your wife, who has obviously forgotten, embarks on a tirade about how awful that particular name is and how no one in their right mind would ever dream of giving their child such a name . . .

You're at a party and accidentally break something small—a glass or a plate—without being seen.

At a party, you sit down on an antique chair and hear it crack. No one else notices.

At the Christmas party held at your boss's house, you accidentally spill red wine on a precious Oriental rug. No one sees it happen.

During the office party held at your boss's house, you accidentally clog up the toilet.

You knock over one of the large pyramid displays of tins at the supermarket. No one sees you do it.

Your umbrella catches on a tablecloth in a large department store and a crystal vase falls over and breaks, but no one sees it happen.

While trying on a white T-shirt in a clothing store, you inadvertently smudge your lipstick on the collar.

While trying on an expensive cashmere sweater in a clothing store, you snag it on your bracelet.

In the middle of the main course of a formal dinner party, conversation is interrupted by the sound of a loud fart from an indeterminate source.

In the middle of the main course of a formal dinner party, conversation is interrupted by the sound of a loud fart you were unable to hold back.

You've invited some friends out for a drink. When the bill comes, you realize you've been slightly overcharged.

You're in a bar having a drink. When your bill comes, you realize you've been undercharged.

Sally has recently begun a job as a nurse in a well-regarded gynecological clinic. Her search for employment has been lengthy, and she is relieved and excited to be finally working in a job she loves for a doctor who is respected in his field and who treats her and the other staff with consideration and generosity.

After a few months happily settling in, she begins to notice what she feels is a pattern. Whenever a young and particularly attractive patient comes in for an appointment, the doctor invariably finds a reason to send Sally out of the room.

You notice that your little boy's gym teacher is always very
physical with him. It makes you feel uncomfortable, but your
son adores him.

Your daughter mentions in passing that the family doctor
had her take her clothes off to check her tonsils.

Your little girl tells you the neighbor put his hand up her
skirt. He and his wife have been friends of yours for years;
his wife is your best friend.

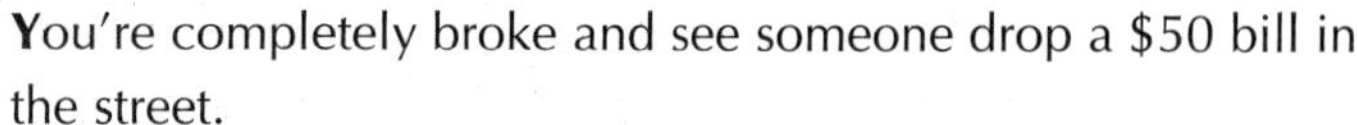

You're completely broke and see someone drop a $50 bill in the street.

You see someone you don't like drop his wallet.

You find a wallet in the street with a considerable sum of money in it. It also has the name, address and phone number of its owner.

You're walking down the street and find a wallet with a considerable sum of money in it but no identification.

You find a gold watch on the washbasin of a public rest room.

You find a wedding ring on the washbasin of a public rest room.

You happen to witness a shoot-out over a drug deal. The two people involved are killed. A briefcase filled with $50 bills and a stash of cocaine is left on the scene of the crime. There is no one else around.

A local bank has been robbed. The thieves escape with the loot, but one bag stuffed with money falls out of the back of the getaway van in front of your house. There isn't a soul in sight.

You suffer sudden impotence,
but the cure guarantees baldness.

Your wife surprises you with breast implants—
a present for your fiftieth birthday. You,
however, loved her breasts as they were and
can't believe she's changed them.

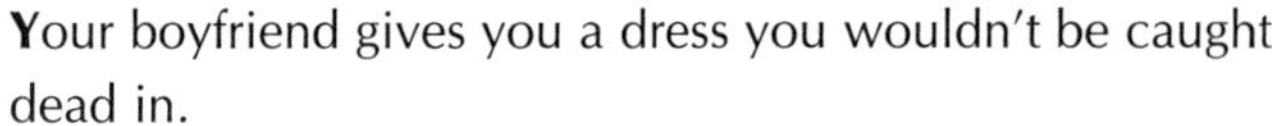

Your boyfriend gives you a dress you wouldn't be caught dead in.

Your boyfriend gives you a really ugly engagement ring, which is a family heirloom.

Your in-laws give you a large item for the house, which you can't stand and can't discreetly dispose of.

An artist friend gives you a large painting, saying it would look perfect in your living room. You hate it.

A friend gives you an explicitly sexual self-portrait.

A friend gives you a birthday present that happens to be the one you gave him last Christmas.

A friend gives you a gift, which you are certain a mutual friend gave her when she got married.

You go to a friend's wedding and put your present on a large table with lots of others. You never receive a thank-you note or any form of acknowledgment.

Sitting on a crowded bus, you notice that the man standing
near you seems to be playing with himself.

The woman standing next to you on the subway seems to
be pushing up against you in what you think is a provoca-
tive way, but it's so crowded you can't be sure.

You accidentally walk in on your friend's husband viewing pornography on the Internet.

You walk in on your friend's son viewing Internet pornography. He claims to have chanced upon it and asks you not to tell his parents.

Your husband comes from a country where it is customary to pierce a girl's ears at birth, and he is adamant about wanting to pierce your newborn daughter's ears. You'd never realized how important this tradition was to him, but you are opposed to it. His family comes for the christening complete with a set of earrings.

Your husband, who is circumcised, wants your newborn son to be circumcised too. You are opposed to it.

Your wife asks you to get a vasectomy.

Your daughter wants to pierce:

* * her nose.

* * her tongue.

* * her nipples.

* * her navel.

* * her clitoris . . .

You find out she already has.

After having an affair with a famous person,
you are offered a lot of money to publish all
the sordid details.

You went out with someone who took
pictures of you in the nude—some of which
are quite graphic—and now he's threatening
to send them to your fiancé and future in-laws
if you don't sleep with him.

The person sitting next to you on the plane stuffs everything she can into her large carry-on bag, including the airline blankets, pillows, headphones, cutlery . . .

The person sitting next to you on a crowded plane takes off his shoes. The smell practically knocks you out.

The person sitting next to you on the plane has nodded off and is snoring like a freight train. It's an eight-hour flight.

You're on a plane sitting next to a couple with a baby whose diaper is in desperate need of changing. You, however, seem to be the only person aware of it.

You decide to splurge and use all your frequent-flyer points to treat yourself to a first-class seat on a long trip. When you board the plane, you discover your seat is next to a woman with a very loud baby.

You've agreed to read a friend's novel but
discover it's awful.

A clairvoyant tells you not to go anywhere near water for at least a year. You had planned to go sailing with a group of friends that summer and have already made all the arrangements.

You're about to board a plane when one of the other passengers tells everyone not to get on, because they have a strong feeling that it will crash just after takeoff.

You see a child dressed in little more than a T-shirt in the middle of winter. He's obviously cold, but his mother doesn't seem to care.

At the playground, you see a mother ignoring her child's dangerous play on equipment designed for older kids.

You see a mother share her cigarette with her very young adolescent child.

You occasionally see a small child at the playground who always has bruises on his face and limbs.

You're sitting in a restaurant next to a couple with a baby. The father casually pours some of his beer into the baby's bottle.

You've been serving on a jury for the past week. The time has come to decide whether the accused is guilty or innocent. The other eleven jury members are unanimous against you and want the ordeal to end.

You're in your dorm room in college, trying to get some sleep, when you hear scuffling and muffled cries coming from one of the other rooms. You finally get up to check it out. The noise is coming from your friend Peter's room.

"Is everything OK in there?" you shout.

"Yeah, everything's fine," he calls back.

But the noise, though not quite as loud, doesn't stop. The following day, it's all over campus—Peter is being accused of date rape, and the girl in question is looking for anyone who can corroborate her story. She claims that someone actually knocked on the door while it was happening and asked if everything was OK . . .

During a war, a few members of your company commit an atrocity.

During a fraternity hazing, a few members start going too far, and the situation begins to get out of hand.

During a war in some faraway place, you are on a scouting mission with a friend behind enemy lines, miles away from your camp. Suddenly, he steps on a land mine and is badly injured. You both know there is no possibility of medical assistance. He asks you to shoot him to put him out of his agony.

You see a close friend's boyfriend kissing another woman.

You see your sister's boyfriend kissing another woman.

You see a close friend's boyfriend kissing another man.

You hear a rumor that your friend's girlfriend is sleeping around.

A close friend is six months pregnant when you discover that her husband has been having an affair with another woman for over a year.

You discover that a friend's husband has been having an affair with another woman who is six months pregnant with his child.

You're in a bar having a drink with a group of friends when you suddenly spot your father kissing a strange woman.

You find out that one of your parents is having an affair. They explicitly ask you not to say anything to the other because it's over and didn't mean anything.

You've been out of work for ages when you pass a club auditioning strippers. You stop in out of curiosity and are offered the job.

Your spouse has been out of work for a while and, after seeing an ad in the paper for strippers, goes along for a laugh and is offered the job.

Your daughter is out of work when she sees an ad for strippers. She and a few friends try out as a joke, are offered the job and take it.

Your friend's wig has slipped a little, but
you're not supposed to know they wear one.

While your colleague is out having lunch, you notice his paycheck lying open on his desk. You've always wondered if he's being paid more than you for the same job.

During a meeting with your boss, he's called out briefly, but tells you he'll be right back. He has been making a list of Christmas bonuses, which he's left on his desk.

You notice someone shoplifting in a supermarket.

You see someone shoplifting in a small local shop.

You've just witnessed a car accident in which the person at
fault is known for being a dangerous and vindictive charac-
ter.

You've just witnessed a car accident in which a good
friend of yours is at fault. Both drivers are looking for wit-
nesses to help plead their case.

Two retired couples have been friends and neighbors for years. Bill's wife, Rose, is bedridden and Meg visits her every day, cheering her up, filling her in on all the local news, bringing her books and magazines. When Meg and her husband go on vacation, Bill waters the plants and feeds the cat. He has little opportunity to go away himself, because of Rose's condition.

When Meg's husband dies, she finds solace with Rose, who comforts and understands her. But to Meg's dismay, less than a month after her husband's death, Bill tries to kiss her. She is shocked and pushes him away. He persists, knowing that she will never tell Rose.

Meg decides to take a short holiday, to let things cool off, but when she returns she senses that he has been in the house, rummaging through her things. He is bolder, and even when she is visiting Rose, she notices him watching her. He suggestively brushes past her in the doorway and whispers obscenities just out of his wife's earshot. One evening when she returns home, she discovers bits of paper with kisses on them pinned to her panties under her pillow.

In a restaurant:

* the family sitting at a table next to yours have children who are insufferably loud and disgusting.

* a couple near you is using offensive language.

* someone within earshot is being incredibly racist.

* the group sitting next to you start having a sing-along at the top of their drunken voices. You were looking forward to a quiet romantic evening.

* you've ordered your food, but before it comes, a dozen rowdy football fans sit down at the table next to yours . . .

A couple you have over for dinner descends into what becomes a heated argument in front of you. They get so riled up they seem to forget that they're not alone, and they bring out all sorts of intimate and nasty things about each other.

You've just found out that your recently deceased grandmother has left you all her money in her will. This comes as
a complete surprise, since your sister, whom you get along
with very well, adored her.

> Your grandmother has left you all her money, but when
> you visited her in the hospital for the last time, she asked
> you to divide it with a cousin you despise.

Your grandmother has left you all her money, but when you
visited her in the hospital for the last time, she told you to
give it all to charity.

> Your grandmother, who has started going senile, hands
> you an envelope with a new version of her will to give to
> her lawyer. You know that up until then you were her
> sole heir.

Your ailing, aged and very wealthy grandfather is being courted by someone who is much younger than him and whose motives you seriously question. He seems quite flattered by all the attention and is in very good spirits. You're the only family member he has let in on his little secret.

An elderly friend passes away and unexpectedly makes you, not his children, his sole heir.

Your mother tells you that, if you don't patch up a very bitter, long-standing argument with your grandfather, he will definitively drop you from his will.

On his deathbed, your grandfather confesses to a terrible crime he committed in the past and got away with.

A friend borrowed $10 and has yet to pay you back.

A friend borrowed $100 and seems to have forgotten all about it.

Last week, your boss borrowed $50 and hasn't mentioned it since.

A colleague invariably avoids picking up the tab.

At a clothing sale, you see a beautiful jacket you'd love to
buy, but someone else reaches for it just before you do. After
carrying it around the shop for a while, they put it down on
a table while they try on something else.

Your all-time favorite store holds an
unprecedented 50 percent-off sale during
your daughter's first piano recital.

A drunk driver pulls into your gas station and slurs, "Fill her up!"

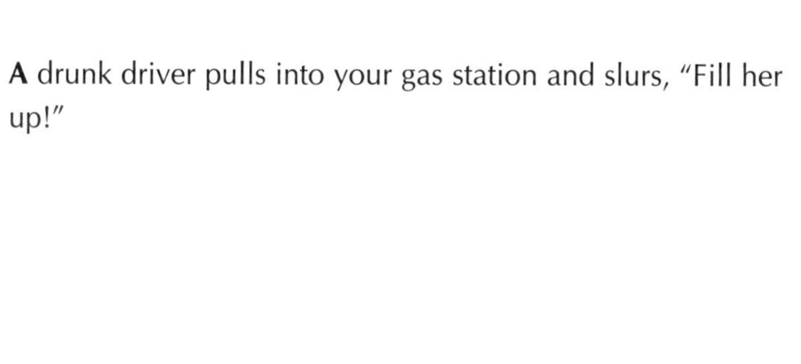

A man who has been drinking steadily all evening at your bar, and who is totally plastered, grabs his keys and staggers out to his car.

You suspect a friend has a serious drinking problem.

Someone (a complete stranger, a colleague, your boss, one of your in-laws, a friend . . .) has:

* a joke sticker on her back.

* his jacket label sticking out of his collar.

* food stuck in her teeth.

* her skirt stuck in her panties.

* newspaper smudges all over her face.

* his fly undone.

* dropped food on his tie during a meal.

* dropped a condom in a crowded elevator.

* dropped a dirty magazine . . .

You're invited to dinner at your in-laws' house. A dish is
served that positively revolts you.

You're invited to dinner at a friend's house. The whole
meal is meat based. You forgot to mention that you were
a vegetarian when you were invited.

You're invited to dinner at a colleague's house. The whole
meal is meat based. You made a point of mentioning that
you were a vegetarian when you were invited.

You're having dinner at a colleague's house and notice
that your glass has lipstick around the rim.

You're having dinner at your boss's house and notice that
the salad, which hasn't been washed properly, has insects
in it.

The next-door neighbor makes an unwanted
pass at you. His daughter is a good
friend of yours.

The neighbors have set up an incredible Christmas-lights display in their garden. It was mentioned on local radio and has started attracting all sorts of people, some from out of town. This has led to traffic jams in the street and noise and disturbance in the evenings. To make matters worse, the lights flicker on and off all night, lighting up your own house and garden like a Christmas tree. Needless to say, the neighbors in question welcome all the attention and may even appear on local television, which you fear will only make matters worse. It isn't even December yet!

At a job interview, you're asked if you want children. You
know it will jeopardize your chances if you say yes.

At a job interview, you're asked if you want children.
You're two months pregnant already, but you know it will
jeopardize your chances if you say so.

Your name is added to a waiting list for an important organ transplant. You realize that, through of someone you know, you could be moved to the top of the list.

Your child is put on a waiting list for an important organ transplant. Your friendship with the director of the hospital would give your child priority over others if you care to use it.

Your child dies tragically in an accident. In the hospital emergency room, the doctors inform you that donating her organs could save the life of another child who has just been brought in.

You see senior partners of your firm light up in a strictly nonsmoking area.

You're interviewing a potential baby-sitter for your child. You want a nonsmoker. She tells you that she smokes, but would never do so in front of the child or in your home. Her credentials are otherwise impeccable.

Though happily married, you have a one-night stand with someone else and discover you're pregnant shortly thereafter. You don't know whose child it is. It's probably your husband's but you can't be 100 percent sure.

You have a fling and get pregnant. Your husband has been away on business for a month, so the baby can't be his. You've been unsuccessfully trying to get pregnant for a number of years.

You are raped and discover you're pregnant shortly thereafter. You don't know whether the father is the rapist or your husband.

Your wife is pregnant. After the initial euphoria, she tells you that she had a one-night stand. The baby is probably yours but you can't be certain.

After letting friends stay at your home for a month while you're away, you return to find that:

* they haven't left a thank-you note or gift.

* they've left your place a mess.

* they've seriously depleted your liquor supply.

* they've broken something small.

* they've run up the phone bill.

* there's no food left.

* something small is missing.

* the plants have died . . .

A friend has asked if he can stay at your place for a few days while you're away on vacation. Your cleaning lady phones to let you know that he's invited friends of his to stay at the house with him.

Housekeepers have always looked after a summer house for you. When you decide to retire there year-round, they leave. Not long after they stop working for you, a number of people phone about the room rental. You assume they've dialed the wrong number, but after a dozen or more similar phone calls, you realize that the housekeepers were renting the place out in your absence.

The couple in the cabin next to yours on a cruise makes love
very noisily every night and shares your table by day.

Some guests staying with you for a few weeks turn out to
be very loud in bed. You've barely slept a wink.

Your grandmother has moved in with your parents, which is working out fine. The only problem is that, whenever your parents want to go on vacation, your grandmother invariably gets ill, ruining their plans. In fact, it has been a long time since they've had a real break. You encourage them to book a holiday abroad, and wait to announce it until just before they leave, offering to spend the two weeks they're away with your grandmother. They agree to the plan. The day after they leave, however, she complains of chest pains, so you rush her to the hospital, where doctors tell you that she has had a mild heart attack, but that she's out of danger. She insists that you call your parents and tell them to come home immediately.

You lend a friend some money and later discover that she made an investment with it that has paid off *big-time*. She only offers to pay you back the original amount, with neither interest nor share in her windfall.

A friend in dire straits comes to you begging for a loan. You learn the following week that he went out and bought something really frivolous with it.

Just before entering your company boardroom to make an important presentation in front of all the big shots, you split your trousers.

An hour before an important dinner with your spouse's new boss, your hairdresser makes you look *totally* ridiculous.

Your son decides to marry someone you can't stand to be in the same room with.

You find a hard-core pornographic magazine under your teenager's bed.

You discover that your adolescent child—who you didn't know was sexually active—is in possession of a half-empty box of condoms.

You discover that your teenage daughter is taking the pill.

Your very young daughter tells you she's pregnant.

During passionate lovemaking, your lover blurts out someone else's name, but subsequently ignores it completely.

During passionate lovemaking, you blurt out someone
else's name by accident. You're sure your partner heard
you, even though they don't say anything about it later.

At a dinner, the topic of infidelity comes up and there's a heated discussion. You know that a number of the people condemning it have been unfaithful themselves.

You have some friends over for dinner. They start talking about abortion and condemn it. You know one of your friends there has recently had an abortion.

People start making slurs against gays at a business lunch. Somebody close to you is gay.

You've prepared a meal for a party, using a small amount of meat stock, completely forgetting that one of your guests is a vegetarian. There is nothing else to eat.

You're cooking for guests in the kitchen, and just as you're about to serve them, you slip and drop the steaks all over the kitchen floor.

The person you are sitting next to at dinner momentarily looks away when you sneeze all over his plate of food.

At a business lunch in a foreign country at which a billion-dollar contract is about to be signed with your company, your host's prize delicacy is served . . . boiled dog.

You walk in on your father wearing
women's clothes.

After buying a lottery ticket for a friend and one for yourself,
you check to see if you've won. Your friend's ticket has won
the jackpot. Although he paid you for it, you'd forgotten to
give it to him, and he has never actually seen it.

You buy a lottery ticket and tell the woman who sells it to
you that you'll give her half if you win the jackpot. You
win the jackpot.

You buy two lottery tickets with a friend. You both agree to give
the other half of whatever you win:

* your ticket wins $100.

* your ticket wins $10,000.

* your ticket wins over $1,000,000.

A friend of yours is about to get married. The date has been set, the invitations sent out, the reception hall reserved, and the presents have begun to arrive. Two weeks before the big day you find out something about her fiancé you suspect she doesn't know:

> * he's bankrupt.
>
> * he gambles heavily.
>
> * he was previously married and has two children.
>
> * he's seeing other women.
>
> * he's seeing other men.
>
> * he's been to prison for armed robbery.
>
> * his first wife died under mysterious circumstances.
>
> * he is already married . . .

Two weeks before a friend's wedding, his fiancée makes a pass at you.

A homeless person comes into your pub, buys a drink and
sits at the bar for over an hour. He minds his own business
but smells awful.

A bag lady picks your shop to settle down in front of on a
regular basis.

You're married to an unsuccessful painter who dies, leaving you a note to burn all his paintings. You love some of them.

A corporate billionaire decides he wants to be cremated with his priceless collection of Van Goghs.

You're in a restaurant with a group of friends, and one person eats twice as much as everyone else. When the bill comes, he says, "Right, let's split it."

A friend you eat with regularly always chooses restaurants—and wine—you can't afford.

Dr. Jennifer M., an eminent psychiatrist, has been treating Samantha for over two years. The young woman was referred to Dr. M. after repeated suicide attempts. She had suffered abuse as a child and invariably ended up in abusive, dysfunctional relationships.

The doctor is pleased with her patient's progress. There have been no further suicide attempts, and Samantha is happier and gaining self-confidence. She also seems to be involved in a much healthier relationship with a man who, though attached, is kind and attentive to her.

The last few sessions, however, have begun to make the doctor feel increasingly uneasy. The more Samantha enters into detail about her relationship with this new man, the more it sounds like her own husband.

A friend's teenage daughter tells you in confidence that:

* she's having an affair with a much older man.

* she's having an affair with a married man.

* she's pregnant.

* she's taking drugs.

* she needs to borrow money to pay a debt.

* she needs to borrow money to pay for an abortion.

* she's about to elope . . .

Your house is on fire and you only have a few minutes
before you have to get out.

There is a fire in your building and you have the choice
of rescuing a valuable painting or a homeless person who
is lying unconscious in the stairwell.

Your building is on fire and you're carrying out an elderly
lady when you realize that she's too heavy and you may not
make it out with her before the ceiling collapses.

While a fire is raging in your building, you realize you
only have enough time to save a cantankerous old neighbor or your dog.

You discover your mother is a kleptomaniac.

Your lover never wants you to be on top.

Your partner can only have sex when they're high.

You discover that your boyfriend has been relying on Viagra.

Your spouse does something amazing in bed for the first time that they must have learned from someone else.

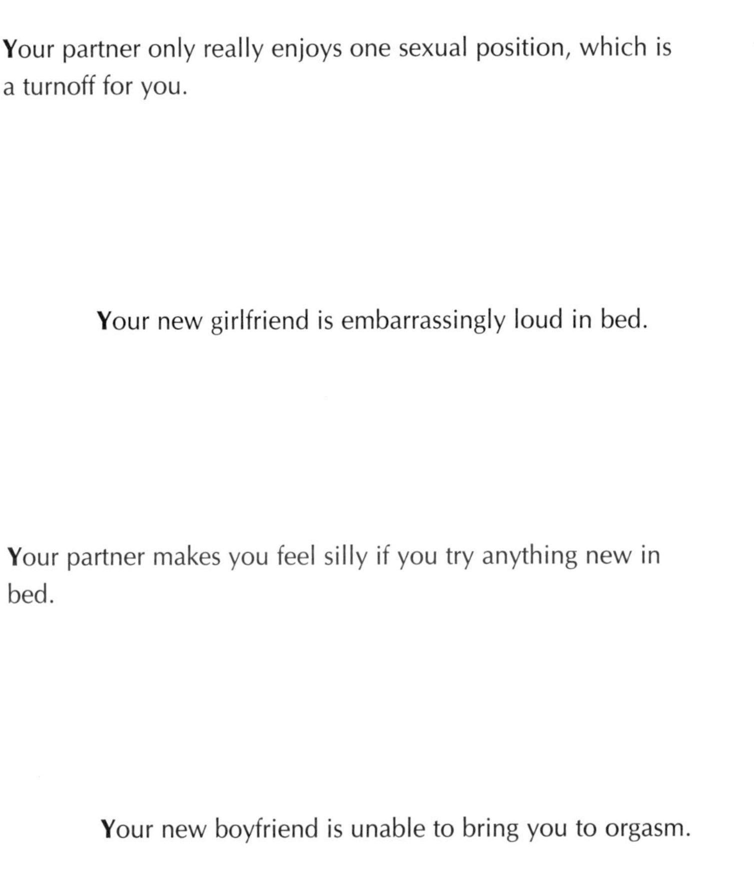

Your partner only really enjoys one sexual position, which is a turnoff for you.

Your new girlfriend is embarrassingly loud in bed.

Your partner makes you feel silly if you try anything new in bed.

Your new boyfriend is unable to bring you to orgasm.

Your fiancé suddenly becomes impotent.

Someone you've never slept with tells everyone what a fantastic lover you are.

You really fall for someone who says they could never be sexually monogamous.

While gossiping with friends about sex and what their respective boyfriends like to do in bed, you realize that yours doesn't do half the things that are mentioned.

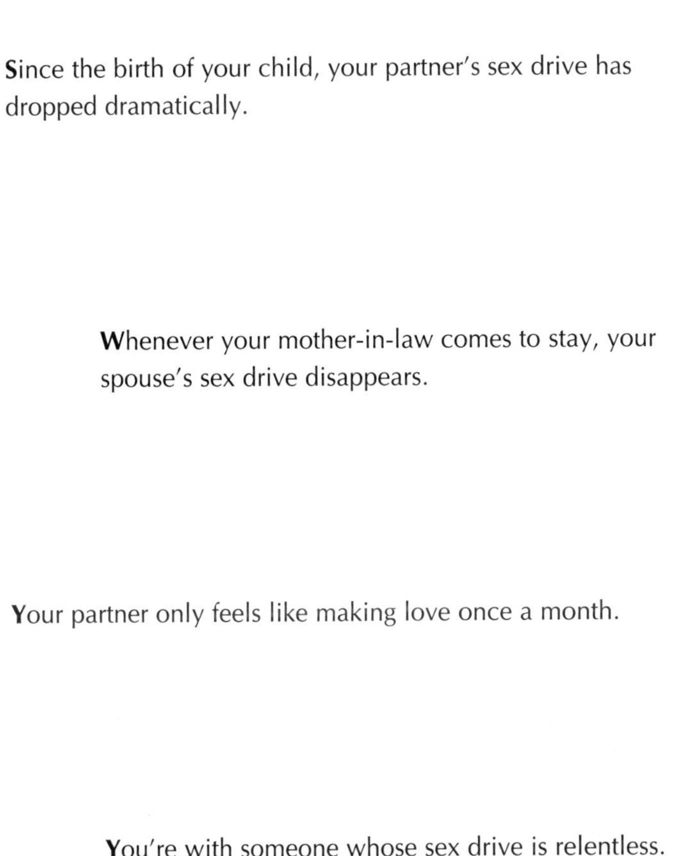

Since the birth of your child, your partner's sex drive has dropped dramatically.

Whenever your mother-in-law comes to stay, your spouse's sex drive disappears.

Your partner only feels like making love once a month.

You're with someone whose sex drive is relentless.

At work, you're assigned the computer terminal of a colleague who's ill that day and inadvertently discover that:

* he's been using it to download pornography.

* he's been using it to look for a job with your company's competitor.

* he's been using it to moonlight.

* he's been sending E-mails with confidential information in them.

* he's received a number of E-mails from a colleague you're interested in . . .

Someone you regularly talk with in an Internet chat room asks to meet you in person.

A friend of yours:

* has an annoying nervous tic.

* says "like" every few words.

* has two or three long dark hairs on her chin.

* picks his nose in public.

* picks her teeth during meals.

* always talks with his mouth full.

* has dandruff.

* has bad breath.

* is always adjusting his crotch . . .

You suspect a woman who has recently
moved into the apartment above yours of
prostitution.

Among the mail you are forwarding to the previous tenant of your new apartment, you notice plain brown envelopes, one of which is torn and reveals what might be child pornography.

The previous tenant's mail still arrives at your door, including literature from an organization called "Citizens for a White America" and "Homemade Explosives Club."

You get pregnant, but you're afraid to tell your parents, because they don't even know you're having sex.

Your boyfriend leaves you before you get a chance to tell him you're pregnant.

Your girlfriend tells you she's pregnant. She knows you're not ready to have children, so you wonder whether you've been "set up." After rummaging around her birth-control pills, you discover she hasn't been taking them.

You're wife was pregnant with somebody else's child when you married her. She asks you never to tell the child.

A good friend who lives in another city phones to ask you a favor. Her boyfriend, George, whom you've met a couple of times and like, is going to be in town overnight for a convention, but he hasn't been able to find a hotel room. Could you possibly put him up for the night? You agree without hesitation; he can sleep on the pullout sofa in the living room.

The night he's in town, he calls and says he'll be coming over in about half an hour and there's someone he'd like you to meet: a woman who's an expert in foot reflexology. Everyone knows you love massage, and he thinks she might be happy to give you one. You agree since it's still early.

When they come over, you find the woman very pleasant, and the conversation easy. You all have a good time. But it's getting late and this woman is making no moves to leave. It turns out that she doesn't live in town either, and that she and George just met at the convention. Finally, around midnight while you're cleaning up in the kitchen, George comes in alone and asks you quietly if you'd mind terribly if she stayed, because she hasn't been able to find a hotel room either and is short of cash.

You are asked by your boss which of two people he should
lay off. The one you dislike is better at their job than the one
you like.

Your firm is considering hiring someone with whom you
had a relationship that ended in a very nasty breakup.
They also have some damaging information about you.

You break a piece of equipment at work, but don't admit it.
Months later, you find out that one of the junior employees
was fired as a result.

Your boss calls you in and gives you a big promotion for
something you didn't actually do.

After you introduce two acquaintances, they decide to start a
business venture together. You later learn that one of them is
shady.

A good friend who works in the financial sector strongly recommends a stock to you. He offers to buy some on his account to speed things up, saying you can pay him back when it's convenient. Two days later, before you've had a chance to pay him, the stock is worthless.

You pass a hot stock tip on to a friend and, since fast action is required, offer him half of the order you've just made. The next day, before he's had a chance to pay you, the company is bankrupt.

You're in the car with your new boyfriend
and his parents. Someone has obviously
stepped in dog poo. The smell is
overpowering.

You're sitting in your car waiting for a friend when a man, presumably mistaking you for a prostitute, offers you money to sleep with him. When he realizes his mistake, he starts to joke with you and offers you increasingly high sums of money. You realize he isn't joking anymore and is willing to pay you:

* $1,000

* $10,000

* $50,000

* $100,000 . . .

At a party, your best friend's boyfriend makes a pass at you.

> **Y**ou wake up one morning after a party in bed with a friend's boyfriend, and you have no idea how you got there or what, if anything, happened when you did. He's still fast asleep.

You're introduced to a friend's new flame. He turns out to be an old boyfriend you broke up with because he was violent.

> **A** close friend confides in you that she really likes this guy and thinks he's interested as well. He has just called you to ask *you* out.

You're at a party and your mother's boyfriend makes a pass at you.

You've taken your young child to a friend's house. One of
the other guests starts telling dirty jokes.

You're having a drink with two friends you've just introduced when one makes disparaging comments about a
minority they don't realize the other belongs to.

You know that a number of the members of your team are taking performance-enhancing drugs. Lately your form has been slipping, and in the last two games, you were replaced halfway through.

You suspect the team doctor is not up front about the contents of the "vitamin" pills he gives the players but no one else seems too bothered. You've just joined the team.

You're mistakenly sent a confidential E-mail revealing that
the company you work for is verging on bankruptcy. None
of the other employees know yet.

Because of a promotion to a senior position, you're given
access to confidential information that the company is
dumping toxic waste.

Jane's current boyfriend broke up with his wife a few years ago. He and Jane have been going out for over a year, and although they spend practically all their time at his place, he isn't ready for her to move in with him. She's really crazy about him and would like there to be more commitment on his part. And although she's uncomfortable bringing it up, she's increasingly bothered by the fact that he still has numerous pictures of his ex-wife with his children in his bedroom while there isn't a single picture of her in his entire house.

Your wife comes home with a new haircut
you can't stand.

You see someone being pickpocketed.

You see someone being mugged when:

* you're alone.

* you're with your mother.

* you're with your partner.

* you're with a group of friends.

* you have a gun in your possesion . . .

A hot new date moves to kiss you. You have oral herpes.

Your boyfriend wants to sleep with you but doesn't have a condom:

* you've never slept together.

* you've been sleeping together for a few months but have never had unprotected sex.

* the only drugstore open is half an hour away . . .

A friend who would like to have a baby but would prefer to avoid the anonymity of a sperm bank asks whether you would be willing to donate your sperm.

A friend who would like to have a baby but whose husband's sperm count is too low asks whether you would mind if she asked your husband to donate his sperm.

At a friend's party, you spot a few CDs that have been missing from your place for so long you'd forgotten about them.
Your friend raves about this great used-music store where
they bought all sorts of good stuff, including these.

You end a friendship after your friend accuses you of
keeping something he lent you. A year later, you find it in
your closet.

Someone gives your child a gift you object to.

Someone gives your three-year-old daughter a toy gun or a set of soldiers.

Someone gives your three-year-old son a doll or a tea set.

You notice two of your little boy's friends make fun of him for playing with a doll.

Your bridge friends are over at your house and begin to joke about your son playing with his dollhouse.

You wish your spouse would lose about thirty pounds but
you know they're really sensitive about it.

You notice that a thin friend almost always disappears for
a few minutes after every meal.

Your children's school has awarded the cafeteria concession
to a fast-food chain you would never take them to.

In a job interview that goes very well, it is clearly implied
that if you lost weight the job would be yours.

Your best friend starts going out with a new man and has less and less time for you. In fact, you rarely get to spend anytime with her at all, and when you do, her boyfriend is always present.

A friend you've known for ages meets and falls in love with a new woman. Whenever you see them together, they always "baby talk" to each other.

You're having trouble getting work as an actress, and you're told
that, if you want to work, you will have to:

* change your name.

* change your hair.

* have all your teeth capped.

* have a nose job.

* have major plastic surgery.

* have breast implants.

* pose for some nude photos.

* sleep with a few people in the industry . . .

In a church, you overhear a man confessing to repeated incestuous "behavior" with his two children. At first, you try not to listen, but you can't help doing so when you realize the nature of his confession. He is ashamed but says he can't help himself. You know that technically the priest is bound by his vows to secrecy and can do very little to intervene in any way. When the man gets up to leave, you catch a glimpse of him and realize he lives in your neighborhood.

Your sister confesses to you that she has committed a murder someone else stands wrongly accused of.

An old friend of the family confesses to you that he was a Nazi war criminal.

One of your parents goes into an irreversible coma without leaving written instructions concerning euthanasia, though they'd always casually said they'd rather die than live like that.

A small child dies of a relatively rare condition, so his doctor
decides to do an autopsy. After a lengthy investigation, he
realizes that the child was given to the wrong parents at birth
and that another boy in his community, whom he knows
very well, is in fact living with the "wrong" parents.

You discover your three-year-old child is not the one you
gave birth to and must have been swapped in the hospital.

You're on your way back from a party one night when you run over your neighbor's cat about a block away from home.

You're driving home on a country road one evening when out of the blue a cyclist swerves into your car. When you rush over to him, you realize you have killed him.

A friend is driving you home in the middle of the night after a party. Suddenly a cyclist comes out of nowhere. Before your friend can swerve out of the way, he hits the cyclist and knocks him over. You both rush over to check if he's OK, but he is dead. Your friend tells you to get back in the car because he wants to drive away as quickly as possible before anyone comes.

You're offered a million dollars to sleep with someone you find absolutely repulsive.

You're offered a million dollars to sleep with someone of the same sex—or the opposite sex if you're gay.

You're offered a million dollars to be a prostitute for one day.

Your elderly neighbors offer you a million dollars to kill a man. He brutally murdered their young child and is about to go on parole.

You are offered a free airline ticket to your chosen destination in exchange for carrying a small package of "documents."

You happen to walk past a colleague napping
on the grass in a public park with other
people around and notice he is inadvertently
exposing himself.

A man comes into the shop where you work to try on a pair
of shoes. His feet smell as if they haven't been washed in
weeks.

You work in an expensive clothing store. Someone comes
in to try on various dresses. She has such terrible body
odor you find it hard to stand near her.

You're an assistant in a department store. A woman comes
in to try on wedding dresses and fixates on the one that
makes her look the worst.

A customer is trying on bikinis in the changing room, and
even though you made it clear she had to keep her panties on, you're convinced she has taken them off.

A friend of yours has told you in confidence that she is HIV positive. After a while, another friend expresses an interest in going out with her.

You fix up two friends, and they surprisingly hit it off. After a while, the closer friend tells you in confidence that he's HIV positive. You had no idea.

You discover by chance that your dentist is HIV positive.

Your child's baby-sitter tells you she's HIV positive.

Your partner tells you they are HIV positive.

A married friend of yours starts having an
affair and wants to use you as an alibi.

You notice some insulting graffiti about you in the school washroom. It looks like it was written by one of your friends.

Something personal comes back to you that you'd only told a couple of very close friends in strict confidence.

A writer friend publishes a story you realize is about intimate aspects of your life.

After helping to get a friend hired by your company, you hear they're after *your* job.

You're having a picnic with a couple who say nothing when their young child begins to play with himself.

While in a restaurant with friends, their little girl misbehaves continuously. They don't react.

You have some friends over to your place, and they say nothing when their child breaks something.

At an adoption agency, you have the final decision in placements.
The case involves a healthy baby for whom there are numerous
applicants, including:

* a childless couple in their twenties.

* a childless couple in their thirties.

* a childless couple in their forties.

* a childless couple of another race.

* a couple with children.

* a lesbian couple.

* a gay couple.

* a single woman.

* a single man . . .

You're on the board of admissions of a good school, where applications always outnumber places. You come to the case of a student who is not academically outstanding but:

* is from an underprivileged background.

* belongs to a minority.

* is a great athlete.

* is the son of a famous person.

* is the daughter of an extremely wealthy family who might make generous donations to the school.

* is the son of a former student.

* is the son of a friend . . .

One of your parents starts getting heavily involved in a weird sect and going off for weeklong retreats. They start neglecting family and friends, dressing oddly and making increasingly large donations to the center.

Your fiancé is much more religious than you and expects you to follow suit.

To marry your current boyfriend, you'll have to convert to his religion.

When you were pregnant with the second of your two children, your husband started spending late nights at the office, which turned out to be the first in a long series of extramarital affairs. Your discovery coincided with the birth of your child and provoked an extended period of depression. You ended up taking pills and then turning to alcohol. Luckily, your family rallied around and got you to a rehab center, where you recovered. They also helped you regain confidence, and you finally have the courage to ask for a divorce. Your husband, however, swears he'll fight you for custody and threatens to use your bouts of depression and alcoholism against you in court.

You book a nonrefundable holiday at a resort, and when you get there, you realize it's a nudist camp.

You and your kids go on vacation with friends who have
children of roughly the same age as yours. You discover they
have a completely different approach to discipline.

You've rented a place with some friends for the summer
and realize that they feed their kids junk food all the time,
whereas you're quite strict about food and your family has
a mainly organic, sugar-free, fat-free diet.

While making love, you realize you could fake orgasm:

* because you're bored.

* to protect your lover's ego.

* to encourage a clumsy, inexperienced lover.

* since your boyfriend is always comparing you to his ex, who had orgasms at the drop of a hat.

* after a marriage counselor tells you it would help matters . . .

You suspect your lover fakes orgasm, but you can't be sure.

A journalist comes across some past dirt on a respected and capable senator. It would irreparably destroy him if it came to light.